D0197202

Spirit Extracts

poems by

Leng Moua

Finishing Line Press
Georgetown, Kentucky

Spirit Extracts

Publisher: Leah Huete de Maines

Editor: Christen Kincaid

Cover Art: Tou Her

Author Photo: Chue Fue Thao, CFT Photography

Cover Design: Elizabeth Maines McCleavy

Printed in the USA on acid-free paper.
Order online: www.finishinglinepress.com
also available on amazon.com

Author inquiries and mail orders:
Finishing Line Press
P. O. Box 1626
Georgetown, Kentucky 40324
U. S. A.

Table of Contents

Alternate Realm

At 35,000 ft,
500 knots through air,
a roaring drag wakes me
from sleep.
My compass-needle spins
to the final approach.
After 18 hours we land
upon a threshold of tongues
unfamiliar cross-
winds whistling engines down,
belts unclick and we funnel
through the portal
to a scribbled language
on sweet and sour menus.
A thick warm morning breeze
slips through sliding doors,
my nose fills with sewage and I
pull my jumper over me
exposing sweat on skin
not prepared to absorb
foreign auras.

Between Locusts and Grasshoppers

"No one ever imagined that these smiley, hoppy things could also be these monstrous destroyers of civilization"
—NPR

Fluttering above waving grass
    we congregate into ravenous swarms
never belonging to grating bark
    and ripe fruit.
        But we are not locusts
    plaguing roots into deserts,
        eating our weight
    when plants are green
        and breeding is spring—instead
we are familiar bodies like
    grasshoppers, solitary
        studying the shape of our wings,
    displaced from our nests
        atop heaven-touching slopes
but not high enough to lose our breath
        or have it stolen from us.
    Our horns are neither long
or short but equal, halved
    like the horns that could not tell us
        body-changing tigers were coming
        or that poppies would be cut
and stories would be told in bloodstains
sewn into cloth.
    Rivercrossings spoke words
    able to close eyes, rot meat.
I am an egg laid on alien banks.
    Evolving beyond my form, my hand reaches
    towards the land and my head turns
    to see what is
        behind me.

Back to the Land

Liquid from boiled-greens
burns the tunnels
of my father's throat.

He sparks a fire
to roast yams under
a clouded crescent,
blood-soiled dripping onto Earth.

A shrouding yellow haze
swells the stomachs of his cousins
and closes an uncle's eye.
We cut bamboo to cradle
their bodies across the river.
Their hands reach through barbed wire
pointing in the direction of my land
while the children have gone off to play.

Flowers Grow on Skin and Bones

> *"Vang Pao, a charismatic Laotian general who commanded*
> *a secret army of his mountain people in a long, losing campaign*
> *against Communist insurgents, then achieved almost kinglike*
> *status as their leader-in-exile in the United States"*
> —New York Times

Can of worms from burrows underneath
mother-ground flesh and limb (shared blood) shrouded
in banana leaves to sleep
sweaty metal burns through
dreams, keeps lids wide.
It's clear through the pall
ornaments have not been harvested.
Wonder-lost in tracks
with no leading hum
of qeej or oxen to accompany the wandering   *plig*, absent of
cockerel steering roads
with morning crows for feet to tread,

      follow.

When I looked back at Loob Ceeb, I cried
because I was leaving my country behind

Open that can of worms that wiggle
through trigger holes. "Overthrow kings"
a spook transcribes coming eye to eye
with the General.
Note: Laotian bin Laden—"to murder thousands and thousands
of people."

...despite of all, one day in the future, if fortunate
I will return to lead the Hmong one more time.

Poppies explode on skin and bones, their pollen
poured into buckets and dumped into caskets.

Apparition

To those who lost their lives while crossing the Mekong River

Wandering eyes never give him pleasure
   the powder smoke
      the smell of burned flesh
         pollute the remembered air

            a river branched of blood
            a torn leg is food for worms
            a scarred hand hunts man

Swishing bushes caused by
   trickling feet, pitches dried from fear pierce
      bedrock of salt formed from the streams of tears
         warranted by families split
      in half or off
     on their own
        metal-death flies to him
          disrupting the still-air
            he has the luck of *yawm saub*
         he is the grey apparition transparent and
         rooted between the two worlds solitude

         in neither black or white

Cut Journey

We are a generation of masks
waiting to be

unveiled. The wind chants names
but we are not

labels. Our language is like water flooding villages
and tones of mountain

songs. Metal in our bones defiles spirits.
The dust beneath our feet will

blow away. Our nectars near-blossom
for eager

bees. Blood will seep through the crevices
of our minds and knives will slice our

tongues. The wind in our lungs is nearly

Bone Layers

Kuv nam offered to tie strings
    of blessings so spirits surrounding me
        would fill the linings of my stomach.

~

    If meat wrapped around your bones, you lived a happy life.

~

    A smiling elder man
    sitting next to my father
    held my hand and proclaimed
    wb ob leeg yog ib yaam.

~

My father's belly sat on his lap like a child.

~

Koj puas noj mov le ma?
(Are you depressed?)

~

Hiding in the shelved boxes were pictures of my father's bones.

I Should Know

Does it just come to me—
language created by wind and blood?
It does not answer only blinks at you.
It is like gazing into a blank page with a
bank of words in my holster,
hoping that they will write themselves.

My father has always been a worker,
a farmer trained by my grandfather. I
wonder if he ever asked questions.
Before ceremonies he'd chant
to air with food offerings.
I could hear Grandfather's name
but never saw him. No,
I don't think Father ever asked questions.

The food present but Grandfather is full.
My father says his spirit also will be hungry one day.
He tells me not to ask how we know.

Suab Ntsov Thaum Tuag (Death Cry)

A choir of chickens singing
in the eyes of death,
a soul regenerated through sacrifice.

Rooster blood drips through
a hole of plastic wrap
sinking into a bowl then,

boiled to make cubes
of dirt-colored foods—*ntshaav*
We dig in like hogs.

We sit in a circle.
We laugh to digest.
We drink to love and respect.

The white man joins us with his
talk of Yexus.
My brothers join him while

our pale father
leaves the table to listen
to the dying hymn.

At the End of the Bed

Sliding in the warm crevices of your
silk skin, telling myself
you must be
what I've been looking for. Our feet
crossing,
bodies molding
nearly becoming one,
I move my hands
across the brown hair
covering half your face,
but then I notice
in your eyes
the shade is not
the same as mine and I
begin to feel our limbs unravel.

Crossing

A child's gaze
wanders beyond me
scribbling the images of blood-stories
and wonderings. Curiosity
lays its hands
on burning metal, sweating skin.
An explosion rips the stomach
outside to in
and the organs sing,
vibrating chords of a
fading generation.
I walk across the bridge
with the child's hand in mine
while *cov nam hab txiv* float below us.

Culture

The sun is woken and my ears
    hear the jingles of finger-bells.

A mix of rice steam
    and incense burns my nostrils
        as the luring chicken crows.

    Split ox horns are flipped;
    it is the language of spirits and ancestors.

Climb chairs and rest on tables
    with bowls of herbs
        and chicken soup.

Relatives tie strings to bless
    to latch renewed souls to our bodies,

    then we drink rounds
    round and round.

The two men at the end
    receive table blessings in cups,
        ay them across the floors of our home.

We eat to welcome the spirits
    into our stomachs.

Afterward, the women pack food for the guest
    and the men circle the spirits to ease,

    and when they have all left,
    and our house is clean,

I take my pen
    and trace outlines
        of letters in the alphabet.

Men Stood

I sit beside a gutted, belly-resting pig
on plastic covered floors; blood of ribs
sinking—heart, liver, intestines—all made to eat.
Nothing wasted unless your surname
was Yang; the belief that eating
hearts would call old ghosts
from cursed love stories.
On the kitchen table, knuckles of my sister
squeeze lime into pepper-sauce.
In the next room, a lady-shaman
hops at the center of her
brown long-board-four-legged chair
as if to touch her head with the ceiling.
In reality, she is galloping
through the spirit world.
Her husband sits behind her
fixed-listening and burning
paper money for the spirits she crosses
and converses with, offering homage
for safe passage. My siblings and I
cannot understand her chants,
but my mother cries. Then, we know
the lady-shaman has met my brother. My father
prepares a rope knotting around
the pig's neck, its soul for promise
of protection and the renewal of ours.
Its end of bargain will birth him
human. My eyes follow pork blood
stream towards the carpet as sounds
of knives chopping on cutting boards
pound me out of this poem.
I stand to join the men dividing meat.

My Mother's Faith

Bumps rose from my skin as blood pumped from her fingertip exposed to air. She claimed the oxygen would contain the bleeding, a science she created over the years. All I could think of was my mother bleeding out on her bedroom floor, a thought pre-determined by her faith in nature. I rushed her to the sink as my chest squeezed. On their own, my hands applied the thick ointment to her split skin. They unwrapped three Band-Aids and with her other hand, we wrapped her finger covering the wound. Unflinching but with a glove, she picked up her knife and continued slicing meat while I stood watching.

Chicken Dinner

From egg to feathers, my father feeds
mushy rice grain to his pets.

In the backyard, they run in circles
chasing their brothers and sisters.

When the batches are laid, my
father takes half for breakfast.

We fill our mouths with
fried rice mixed with babies.

After licking our spoons we dip our manners
into the soup and take a piece of chicken.

We tear meat from the bones
and drown it in *kua txob*.

We fill the spaces
in our teeth with eyes and skin.

The head of our household
eats the head of their household.

Its beak contorted,
I spit my bird onto the plate.

Calling Them to Come Eat

I summon to the podium
my grandfather whose spit
dripped into the bowl of his flute

uncork the hole

let it leak

the spirits of past generations
who knew the leaves decomposed
into their grave-mounds
on the highest hills
keeping watch over visitors
offering spirit money and incense
for their homes in the sky.

My grandfather I hardly knew
but aunts and uncles compared our faces
and the music he achieved.

I am his shared-blood child
extending an unfamiliar legacy
to aliens whose Fathers call me alien.

Peeling scabs from my face
and coloring the festered scars
carved by my nails

covering the pits I am to fall in
remembering his blood-drained corpse
his lingering spirit
I summon to the podium.

Domestic Issues

Do not pull me from
    the ledge if below are tongues
        cut from the mouths of

            my brothers and sisters.

Let me fall and emerge with
    a handful, lay them next
        to our dirt-feet,

            compare loss of colors.

Those with fists and ideas
    look pale avoiding the sun,
        sleeping with thirsty bats

            and men's wives and women's husbands.

Offered to our mothers
    are knuckles and bullets
        that sew the flower cloth

            hiding behind their closed lips.

Purple poppies
    grow from pores
        and their roots break bones

            splintering a shaded voice.

We have left ways
    of the old land but still
        on our knees

touching forsaken ground.

Jetlag

Green fields and slopes
        like Father's stories,
          these mountains do not breathe
    the air from home.

I follow paved trails
    and tree-shadows arch over the path.

    I forget the language gripped
in the ground until words

within my blood are heard under
    a *tsev teb* built by uncle where hands sorted

    earth's offsprings.

Standing on
    the motherland where

    blood seeped into her roots
and dispersed down river,

body splits and I am
    back home, up since last night,

my mother facing out the doorway
    chant-calling my spirit to return.

Notes

"Flowers Grow on Skin and Bones": (*Qeej*) is a Hmong flute made of bamboo and wood that is used during funeral ceremonies. The Hmong believe that the songs played by the instrument are meant to lead the deceased to their rightful place in the afterlife. These songs can also be directly translated into speech. The translation for (*plig*) is spirit. (*Loob Ceeb*) is the Hmong pronunciation of Long Cheng which was a Laotian military base that served as a town and an airbase where many Hmong resided. It was also the place where General Vang Pao said his last goodbyes to his people before fleeing from the invasion of the NVA to come to the United States.

"Apparition": (*yawm saub*)—God

"Bone Layers": (*kuv nam*)—my mother; (*wb ob leeg yog ib yaam*)—both of us are the same; (koj puas noj mov le ma?)—Are you even eating at all? This question is usually asked to others as a euphemism to gauge their current well-being in life.

"Suab Ntsov Thaum Tuag" (Death Cry): (*ntshaav*)—refers to blood and sometimes used as a name for a dish made of blood; (*Yexus*)—Jesus

"Crossing": (*cov nam hab txiv*)—the mothers and fathers

"Chicken Dinner": (*kua txob*)—pepper sauce

"Jetlag": (*tsev teb*)—a farmhouse with only a roof and no walls that is built next to farms which provided a place to rest and sort crops

Leng **Moua** is a poet from Central Valley California. Born to Hmong immigrant parents from Laos, he is part of the second generation of the Hmong population living within the United States. He studied at CSU Sacramento and received his BA in English. Currently, he resides in his hometown of Merced, CA.

CPSIA information can be obtained
at www.ICGtesting.com
Printed in the USA
LVHW031504150821
695369LV00003B/382